LEARN

FROM YOUR

LENDER

Sean Antonius (NMLS #1552487)

425.681.8075

SeanAntonius.com

Equal Housing Lender

To the best of our knowledge, the information contained herein is accurate and reliable as of the date of publication; however, we do not assume any liability whatsoever for the accuracy and completeness of the below information.

Any information given in this book should not be mistaken for legal advice. It is the customers' responsibility to determine which mortgage program would suit your needs the best.

"Home is the nicest word there is."

- Laura Ingalls Wilder

To the Wife and kiddos! Kaylene, Jackson, Sydney, Kaeden, Gavin and lil' Dempsey... Your ability to support and encourage me through all of my insane ideas is the only reason any of them take flight...

Sean

Table of Contents

1. Know The Difference Between Different Types Of Homes You Can Purchase

When you're a first-time homebuyer and you're looking to escape the apartment life, you decide to head out and start to look for a home to purchase. Well, it's helpful to know the different types of properties that exist.

Simply speaking, there are four main types of properties.

Each property type has pros and cons. Which type that you focus your search on will be dictated by your lifestyle, family size, and the goals you're trying to accomplish. Let's take a deeper look at the four different types of homes you can purchase. (Obviously these don't constitute ALL of the options available... but for our purposes here, they will start our conversation.)

Single Family Home

The first is a single-family home (also known as a "detached" home). This is the most common type of home purchased. It's what you're used to seeing in a neighborhood where it's a detached home, typically with a garage and there's going to be at least a little space in between each house.

This is the most common type of home purchased in America, making up 82% of all homes purchased in 2019 (NAR). Of those detached homes purchased, 14% were New Construction and 86% were "resales". It's the kind of place that people will purchase when they think about the "American Dream" but it is not the only type of property.

Condos

The second most common type of property is a Condominium. A Condo is similar to an apartment however everyone in the complex owns their unit, yet shares the ownership of the rest of the property.

With a condo, you own everything inside your walls. Technically you own the airspace. Everything outside your walls is either common space, owned by somebody else, or belongs to the complex itself.

When you own a condo, you're likely going to have a condominium association fee every month or every year.

These fees will cover things like your shared amenities, taking care of the parking lots, landscaping common areas and parks, maintenance of shared structures, paint, roof repair, any needed security, etc.

Condos are an excellent option for people who want to be in a close environment, have the security of ownership, and don't wish to have the sole responsibility of maintaining a yard or overseeing many of the needed upkeep items you'll have to manage owning your detached home. They are also typically less expensive than their detached counterparts.

Townhomes

The third type of property we'll touch on is a Townhome.

A townhome is similar to a condo in that you have shared walls, but with a townhome you own everything inside of your unit as well as the front and back of it.

Also, you typically see that the property (actual physical land) is owned with a townhome.

Most townhomes are going to be 2-3 stories with a small front yard and/or backyard. Occasionally, you will see townhome complexes that also have attached or detached garages.

Duplex

The fourth type of property is a duplex.

A duplex is a unit that has two homes attached in the middle.

Typically, if you own a duplex, you're going to own the entire unit and either live in one unit and rent the other, or rent both units out as an investment property. In some areas you may be able to buy only one half of the duplex as well, similar to the Townhome option above.

In that case, you would own everything inside your unit as well as your yard with one shared wall with your neighbor.

2. Ask To See Any Homeowner's Association Documents Before You Make an Offer or During Your Inspection Period

It's really important to know what's required before you buy into a neighborhood or choose to let yourself be "governed" by a Homeowner's Association (HOA). Every homeowner's association or HOA is a little bit different in what they allow and what they don't allow, and they typically detail all of their "rules" in a recorded document called the Covenants, Conditions and Restrictions (CC&R's).

HOA documentation can have differing requirements of each homeowner and also different association dues… so you'll want to know all of these things BEFORE you move into a neighborhood.

Let's say for example you own a motorhome you'd like to park; you work on cars at your home, or you'd like to paint your home a certain color. You'll want to read the HOA documents to make sure that all of things that are going to be "non-negotiable" for you are all acceptable options.

Some neighborhoods may not allow motorhomes and you'll have to put it in storage. They may require you to obtain permission from the HOA board regarding exterior paint colors, or have "aggressive breed" restrictions for pets. All of these things can add or diminish your desired use and enjoyment of the property, so it's important that you have the opportunity to review the CC&R's prior to submitting any offers.

Sometimes a review prior to your offer is not possible so you can review the documents during your inspection period and have a contingency in place that allows you to rescind your offer if you run across any "deal breakers" in the neighborhood rules. When exercising any of your included contingencies within their agreed upon time periods... you will receive your Earnest Money back.

What's Earnest Money?! Keep reading.

3. Find Out If You Qualify For Any Special Financing Programs

One of the many reasons that it's important to talk with a lender before you start going out and looking at houses is so that you can know exactly which mortgage programs you qualify for and how much home you can afford based on the payment range that fits best with your budget.

There are some special programs (both government and/or lender specific) that can make it easier for renters to become homeowners as well as people selling and moving up (or down).

The **VA Loan Program** is a great example.

VA stands for Veterans Administration and this is a loan that is available for most veterans and active duty military.

There are some requirements, so you'll want to speak with a Loan Officer to make sure that you do qualify. They can also help you get the Certificate of Eligibility from the VA showing that you qualify and what terms, exemptions, entitlement amounts that you qualify for all based on your service and disability details.

The VA loan is really one of the most impressive loan programs that is offered as it a) requires no Down Payment, b) requires No PMI, and c) has VERY competitive rates, even as borrowers have less than ideal credit scores... all as a thank you for your service.

In addition to that, we (and many others) offer additional discounts and benefits for VA borrowers in the form of closing cost discounts and cash rebates from Realtor commissions. My team specifically, we do this through a program called Homes for Heroes. This same program also has the same discount and rebate benefits for 1) Teachers, 2) Healthcare professionals, 3) Police, 4) Firefighters/EMT, and 5) Corrections officers. Reach out to us directly for more information about the Homes for Heroes program!

Another type of special program is the **FHA Program**.

This was designed for homebuyers to be able to bring only a small down payment at closing and still get competitive interest rates with less than stellar credit.

In most cases, the FHA program only requires a 3.5% down payment compared to a normal conventional home loan that requires a 5 or 20% down payment depending on qualifications and geographic area. It is a short-term solution to get into homeownership as it does have a down side. It has a PMI premium that last quite a long time! Not to worry though, as you can always refinance down the road when your situation changes or the Equity position in your home has improved.

The next loan is a government program that helps home buyers get into a house with little or no money out of pocket and it is called the **USDA Program**.

This was designed for rural communities and typically is available in more "country" areas.

This program is great for those homebuyers because it also does not require a down payment and provides 100% financing.

The downside to USDA? Typically lower DTI ratios ceilings, typically lower income cap and typically longer closing timelines.

There also maybe some **local grants** available that you qualify for. In the area that I work in (Washington state and the greater Puget Sound area) we have a program that covers your typical down payment on a conforming first loan. This program loans you the down payment coverage for your first mortgage and essentially becomes a 2nd mortgage. This second mortgage is still due at the end (balloon) but it is "silent" in that it sits dormant with no accrued interest and requires no payments on it until your first mortgage is paid off. It's a decent option for those buyers wanting a zero down payment purchase loan but cannot qualify for a VA or USDA.

You'll want to speak with a local professional to find out if you qualify for any grant programs that currently exist. As there are a few "downsides" to this program as well. Quality guidance and education is KEY when considering programs like these.

These programs can and do change fairly quickly as often times the money is limited and will run out depending on how, where and when those aid funds and special programs are allocated.

So, if you find out you qualify for a grant program you should move quickly while the money is still available.

4. Be Prepared To Act Fast When You Find What You Want

***Important! Working with a reputable, experience and professional Real Estate Agent is KEY on this point!

You do not want to delay in putting an offer on a home when it meets your needs and you feel like it's the one for you. "If you sleep on it, you MAY not sleep IN it." Some areas of the country may not move as quickly in terms of a home's number of days on the market... but in my market and many others, you have to be prepared to jump quickly when you find a home that fits for you.

Also, depending on the market (price points, inventory, supply vs. demand, etc.) there is a good chance your offer will go up against other offers for the same home. The Listing agent will collect all offers and then present each offer to the homeowner and discuss the pros and cons of each one.

There's no reason to wait in getting your offer in as fast as possible to have the best chance at being the only one they're looking at. Often times your offer can implode an offer review date and just be attractive enough for the seller to not wait for more offers to come in.

When a seller receives an offer from a buyer, they have three options to choose from:

1. They can accept the offer

They can take your offer exactly the way that it has been presented and they can execute the contract.

2. They can do nothing

The seller can receive your offer and they can never respond or even acknowledge that they received your offer. There's technically no legal requirement for them to respond to your offer.

Now obviously in most cases, the seller will respond, but understand it's not a requirement.

3. They can counter your offer

The most common outcome is for a seller to either counter or accept your offer.

If they do counter, it could be regarding the price, but they could also counter on any other terms within your offer. The most common terms that get a counter-offer are a) size of the earnest money, b) the escrow/title company that will be used, c) the closing day, d) the inspection period and so on.

So again, it's critically important that when you do find a house that you're interested in and you want to buy it, you move quickly to purchase that home.

Shameless self-promotion: BE PRE-APPROVED! There is nothing worse than losing a home that you want because you went shopping for homes, found a home that fits you and your family... and THEN you needed to spend the next day or two getting your finances/loan documentation and approved loan scenarios in order just to find out that another buyer got that home under contract. This happens ALL THE TIME in my market and can easily be avoided if you take care of that stuff prior to home shopping.

5. Most Buyers' Agents Represent You For Free

We'll often get the question - how is it possible that home buyer agents can represent a buyer and not get paid?

Well, they do get paid.

The fees/commissions paid to the buyer's agent for bringing you as the buyer and representing you in the transaction are most often paid by the seller from their net proceeds when the home closes.

When a person lists their home for sale, they sign a listing agreement with that agent.

The listing agreement will cover all of the terms such as the listing price, how long are they going to work together and what the commission will be for BOTH agents involved in getting the home sold a new owner.

So, let's say for example, the seller agrees to pay 6% commission. That listing broker gets to decide how to split the commission. Typically, the listing agent will keep 3% and offer 3% to the agent who represents the buyer.

The buyer's agent is being taken care of by the commission that the seller is paying.

6. Get Pre-Approved For A Home Loan Before You Start House Hunting

I touched on this briefly in a previous chapter… but it's so important that it deserves its own full section of the book! It's really important before you go to look for your new house that you know what you are qualified for. Price ranges, preliminary interest rates, monthly payments (including things like taxes, insurance, PMI and any HOA dues) are critical for you to know BEFORE you go falling in love with a home.

You'll avoid situations like the following: You go and find the home of your dreams and you put in an offer that's accepted by the seller. Then, come to find out a few weeks later that you don't actually qualify for that amount of house and that you'll need to go find a smaller home. This is why you should always get pre-approved with a reputable lender before you go out looking at houses.

Being pre pre-approved means that you will know exactly how much home you qualify for as well as the likeliest terms, rates, payments, etc. that you'll encounter.

7. Understand The Home Buying Process Before You Start

There are basically seven steps to buying a house you'll want to understand. The Home Loan process parallels this, with some subtle additions and nuances so I'll detail that process in the next section.

I'm going to share the process in detail so you will always know where you are at any given time once you make the decision to start the road to becoming a homeowner, and what to expect along the way.

Step 1. Get Pre-Approved

We just talked about how important it is to get pre-approved so you will know exactly how much home you're qualified for and what your payment will be on any given house.

Being pre-approved will also strengthen the offers later when you go to write that contract because the seller will have confidence knowing you've already been pre-approved for the home loan. In the market that we work in, this is essentially required for your offer to even be considered and presented.

Why would a person who is selling their home, enter into a contract with someone to buy it if they weren't confident in that person's ability to perform and actually complete the transaction with the proper financing.

This process (and letter that you include in your offers) assures the seller that a local, reputable lender has fully vetted your assets, bank accounts, employment history & income as well as your credit history, scores and debt loads.

Writing and submitting offers without this step being completed is essentially a waste of time for everyone involved... including you.

Step 2. Find The House

Next, you're going to hire a real estate agent. They will help you in finding the perfect house, represent you in your contract writing and negotiating, and carry Errors and Omissions insurance to cover contract errors.

Your Realtor has access to every home on the market and even houses that you might not be able to find on Zillow, Realtor.com or any other websites.

These are called "pocket listings" so ask your Realtor if they know of any. These aren't legal in all areas so make sure to ask about the specifics of your search area.

Some things to consider when deciding on which agent you'll hire and allow to represent you (this is a big deal after all):
- Experience (not in years! In number of transactions!) – who carries more value? One who's been in the business for 10 years but does 3 deals per year, or one who's been an agent for two years, but has done 40 transactions per year?)
- Availability – Are they full time or part time?
- Responsiveness – How quickly and easily are you able to get ahold of them?
- Personality – you could potentially be spending quite a few hours with this person... are they easy to be around?
- Education – Are they just filling in the blanks on the pre-written forms and having you sign, or are they full explaining each

section and all of your protections/potential pitfalls within the contract?

- Negotiation prowess – Will they fight for you? Will they negotiate on your behalf or do they just fold and suggest total agreeance for fear of losing their commission or having to lose a contract and go out to show you more homes? Or do they truly know when to tell you that these numbers are great and this is a good deal?
- Reputation amongst their peers – Do they have a good or a bad rep in the local market? This could affect you down the road.
- How well do they know "homes" – General knowledge about homes, layouts, construction, deficiencies, cost of repairs, etc. Do they KNOW what they're looking at when they're inside a home with you?
- Are they on the same page with you? Did they take the time to fully understand your wants and needs in a home, ask you your timeline, etc. Or are they just interested in slamming you into ANY home as quick as possible?
- Did you just randomly run into an agent at an open house?
- DO NOT post on a community Facebook page asking for a Real Estate Agent or

Lender referral! You'll have 1,324 comments on your thread in 8 minutes. Ask trusted friends or family for a referral instead.

Remember that you've likely never done this before (or possibly once or twice in the past). You MUST take the time necessary to ensure you have an advocate on your side through the finding/offering process and that they have YOUR best interests in mind... not their own.

IF they can't immediately answer any/all of the above questions with enough confidence to make you feel comfortable in partnering with them... keep looking.

Step 3. Write an Offer and Get "Under Contract"

Once you find the house that you want to purchase, you're going to write an offer to that seller. Often referred to as a "Purchase and Sale Agreement" (or PSA).

This is the "beginnings" of a contract, but it's only signed by you, not by the sellers yet.

On the offer, you will include your offering price, when you want to close and take ownership, how much money you want to put up for your down payment and Earnest Money and all the other parts of your offer will be listed on the contract.

Again, a great real estate agent will be able to detail the ins and outs of each part of this agreement so you fully understand where you're protected and the timelines associated with each of those protections.

It is called an Executed Contract once the seller accepts and signs it. This is also commonly referred to as "Mutual Acceptance" and typically counts as "Day ZERO" on most of the timelines moving forward.

Step 4. Get a Home Inspection

You're going to want to hire a 3rd party independent inspector to come in and go through the house. They will tell you what they find out is right and wrong about the house. You have the opportunity to attend this inspection, and you should.

A good inspector will consider it their job to point out everything that's wrong with the home as they inspect every single inch with a "fine-tooth comb" to find every tiny imperfection.

NOTE: The "imperfections" that they uncover will likely be MANY. That does NOT mean the house is not worthy of you buying it. Obviously any larger than normal, or even VERY large and catastrophic items will need to be addressed by someone.

Great inspectors will give you a full report of their findings along with the detail of each and their opinions on the severity of each... big deal or small deal?

You have to really be purposeful with what you decide is important and fixable in the future during that inspection period. This is NOT your opportunity to be super nit-picky about every little thing in the report. Consider those things a normal "to-do" list for any homeowner. That's the FUN STUFF of homeownership.

Try to only address larger than normal items with your agent and the sellers.

Obviously, the above opinion is only my own... some realtors may disagree with that approach and suggest that you be super "nit-picky" with your inspection items... to each their own, I guess.

Step 5. Home Appraisal

This will be ordered from your mortgage company. This is an independent 3rd party who is approved by the lender you're working with who will come out to the house that you're purchasing and assess its value.

The actual in-person inspection that they perform is very quick and designed to look for latent defects, safety hazards or code violations... they are NOT a home inspector assessing the home's condition and need for improvements/repairs. They will then use comparable sold homes in the area within a certain amount of time to determine the VALUE of the home you're purchasing. The bank requires this process to determine if the home you're buying is WORTH what you're agreeing to pay for it. The bank is essentially taking stacks of HUNDREDS of THOUSANDS of dollars off of their vault shelf and handing it over to the seller on your behalf. They want to ensure that the asset they're loaning on is worth the money. Makes sense.

As long as the value that the appraiser gives the house is above or equal to your contract price, then your mortgage company is going to give it the thumbs up.

If for some reason the home comes in at a lower opinion of value, either you'll need to renegotiate the contract or you may need to pay the difference out-of-pocket. You also have the option to stop the contract, not buy the home and receive your earnest money back.

Step 6. Receive Full Loan Approval

This will let you know that you've been completely approved and you're ready to go to closing. An underwriter that works for the lender you're borrowing from has reviewed the entire transaction from top to bottom and made certain that it all aligns with the loan guidelines for the program/loan that you're getting.

Everything has been done in terms of researching your credit, income, and background. Receiving Final Approval means that the mortgage company feel confident in providing you with a home loan.

This is also the time where the documents for your home loan and all the papers that you're going to have to sign with the Closing Agent/Escrow are going to be drawn up and those are going to be sent to the closing company.

Step 7. Attend Closing & Become The Owner

Now it's time to attend closing, sign all the paperwork and you will officially become the new homeowner. There are two VERY important documents in this giant stack of papers. One is the Note. This is you promising to pay back the money you've borrowed from the Bank. The other is the Deed. This is the document of ownership that is recorded with your county or city officials that makes you the owner of record.

Closing is also when you will provide your down payment and any other funds that you are paying along with any other minor fees that come up along with purchasing a home.

Then... KEYS!

8. Keep An Open Mind

When we say keep an open mind, what we want you to do is to know what's realistic for your budget.

If you have a $100,000 budget, that's going to purchase a different kind of home than a $300,000 budget and that budget will purchase a different home than a $500,000 budget.

Neither one of those is right or wrong, but you have to understand what's realistic for your price range.

One of the exercises that can be helpful is to do a "needs" versus "wants" sheet side-by-side.

Take a piece of paper and make one column for needs and one column for wants. List out things like the number of bedrooms, bathrooms and different features you need vs. want. Layouts, neighborhoods, school districts, and size of garage are all the things that you need to assess. What do you feel are important about the house that you're going to go shopping for? Now, Stop reading. Make a list. I'll wait.

Now that you have your list, take a hard look at it, shuffle some stuff around… negotiate with your spouse and then settle on your finalized items. Now look at your list and compare it to what I call the HGTV effect.

These shows about buying houses on HGTV (or renovating with the Chip's and Jo's of the world) have made some buyers not fully understand the actual process.

Any time you have any questions at all or you want to talk about why the homes you're touring are not meeting your criteria… have that conversation with your real estate agent. Their job is advocating for you in all things home shopping! If they don't fully understand your wants vs. needs in the search criteria of homes you're seeing, then you haven't even left the starting block yet.

9. The Home Loan Process

Step 1. Pre-Approval

After your initial Loan Application is taken, Your Loan Originator will review your income, credit and assets to assess qualification. Initial documents will also be collected, which could include: paystubs, W2's, Tax Returns, Bank/Retirement Account Statements, and more.

Step 2. Purchase Offer Accepted

Between the pre-approval process and this stage, the Loan Process will stall for a bit as you will be working with your Real Estate Agent to find a home. Once you find a home and sign a Purchase and Sale Agreement, the Loan Process will begin again.

Step 3. Updated Documentation

At this point we will collect updated items to be reviewed by the lender's underwriting department. This list again may include, but is not limited to: paystubs, W2's, tax returns, assets, etc. You'll also want to start gathering up insurance quotes for your Home Owner's policy.

Step 4. Disclosures

There will be MANY emails flying around from ALL
the different players in the process at this point.
Keep your chin up and handle each request or
piece of information ONE AT A TIME… and DO
NOT hesitate to ask questions if you don't
understand something!

A set of initial disclosures will be sent from your
Lender. These are various documents that give the
lender permission to move forward with lending
you money. There will likely be a set that will be
required to be printed and signed with a pen,
while there will also be a set that has the option
to be signed electronically.

Step 5. Processor Review

Once all initial documents are given to your loan
originator's office, the processor will then review
and request any additional documentation that
may be needed. It's their job to present a nice,
neat, clean package to the bank's underwriter to
ensure the smoothest process possible.

Since the processor has the most communication
with the underwriters and has the best
understanding of documents that are needed,

they will more than likely have additional items needed and will reach out periodically to get them.

Step 6. Loan Submission

Once all of the documentation is received by you and various third parties, your loan will be submitted to underwriting. Typically, within a few business days, initial loan approval should be issued.

Step 7. Initial Loan Approval

The underwriter will review your application and all documents provided and then will issue an initial loan approval. There will almost always be additionaldocuments requested though... Items that will typically be needed and not completed yet are HO Insurance documents, likely additional bank statements and satisfactory Appraisal documents.

Step 8. Loan Resubmission

Once all underwriting conditions are met, our processor will resubmit all the documents and conditions provided... to be reviewed by underwriting once more.

Step 9. Final Loan Approval

The underwriter will review your application and documents again to ensure that all of the loan conditions requested have been met, then issue a final loan approval.

Step 10. Final Documents at Escrow

Coinciding with the above step of that Final Loan Approval, the underwriter will issue a "Clear to Close" (there are no sweeter words to a Lender's ears)!

The Bank will then draw up, prepare and send the final loan documents to your escrow/closing company. Once escrow completes their preparation, they will reach out directly to you to schedule a signing appointment and provide all the information regarding the final dollar amount needed for closing, if any.

Step 11. Loan FUNDED!

Once fully signed documents have been received back at the lending institution, depending on whether you're purchasing or refinancing, your loan will fund (bank will send escrow a wire for the loan amount) and the transaction will then close within 24 hours to 4 business days.

10. Keep Your Money Wherever It's At

If you have "money in the mattress", aka, cash that you'd like to use in a purchase transaction… you'll want to get that money in the bank at least 2 months ahead of when you want to purchase a home.

There's a term we use called "seasoning" in which you're going to have to season that money if you want to use it for a down payment or anything that has to do with purchasing a home.

If the money is not seasoned, the mortgage company will definitely ask you to prove where it came from. Unseasoned CASH cannot be used in a real estate transaction. They do not want to see any large deposits into your account without being easily trackable and sourced.

This of course doesn't include your normal paychecks, child support or any other money you receive on a monthly basis. But more so, large deposits that are harder to explain.

You should also know that the mortgage company will probably look at your bank accounts in the beginning of the transaction but there's also a chance that they could look again right before closing. (STRONG Chance…)

So, don't try to be sneaky and add $10,000 or whatever amount into your checking account right before closing. You could lose the loan approval if they go back and look at your accounts again and see something totally unaccounted for or out of the ordinary.

Before doing anything with your funds… consult your lender or escrow closing company to get specific instructions on HOW to move money around, or whether it's even necessary. Don't assume.

11. Six Things NOT to do in a Mortgage Transaction

You would think that most of these things Go Without Saying… but you'd be surprised how many clients we've had who have done one or more of these things not knowing it would severely impact the process… So, I STILL TELL EVERYONE!

1. Don't Quit Your Job.

The Lender is looking for employment stability and will need to verify your present employment as part of the approval process. Some people assume that once this is done in the beginning of the process, you're good to go!

What people forget is this: Someone from the Bank's compliance department is going to CALL your stated employer the day before Closing and ask them if you still have a job there.

Seriously bad news if that person says No!

2. Don't Acquire New Debt.

Don't buy a new car, open a new credit card or finance new windows for your home you haven't even bought yet. New tradelines or increased debt load can severely impact your loan approval. This is not a "hard and fast" rule... It MAY BE OK to buy a new car if it's needed. Just don't do it without asking your lender FIRST!

3. Don't Shop Around for Loans, Cars or Anything Else.

The time for shopping rates and lenders is BEFORE you're under contract, or for ONE OR TWO days RIGHT at the beginning of your loan starting... Once you pick a lender, stick with them. Having your credit pulled too many times within a certain time frame can slightly reduce your scores... we don't want that.

4. Don't Deplete OR Move Your Assets.

Your Approval is, in large part, is based on the lender's verification of income and assets! So, after loan approval, don't deplete or move any of your money around without asking the lender or processor HOW and WHEN to do it.

5. Don't Relocate or Pack Information into boxes or Storage units that might be needed for Your Loan.

Self-explanatory I think?!

6. Don't Stop Paying Your Current Mortgage or Any Bills.

Also, fairly Self-explanatory...

12. Start Online But In The End, Trust A Real Person

84% of today's Home Buyers (and climbing) start the home buying process online.

They look for homes online, they research different mortgage programs; it's a normal thing in today's age and totally OK to do! One thing to know is online information can be outdated or even incorrect so try not to "correct" your Lender or your Real Estate Agent with something you think you know because you read it online.

The Internet is the Bathroom Wall of Society… ANYONE can write ANYTHING on it.

There's no requirement or oversight on websites nor any of the information that exists online. Whatever you find online, in the end, you want to find a local professional to help you understand that information and how it pertains to you exactly.

In terms of finding a home, the same thing is true.

It's fine to start online with your home search (NOT Zillow though! Ugh…) but in the end you want to find a Realtor that you trust and work with them. A local Realtor is also going to potentially know about homes not available online or that are ABOUT to be listed. Realtors will have relationships with other agents and this can help you find homes that may not be available YET online.

It may also help you get the contract if you get into multiple offer situations, so it's important to start your search online but in the end trust local professionals.

PRO TIP: Get a copy of the Purchase and Sale Agreement BLANK ahead of time to read it. I mean, why would you NOT do this?!

13. Visit The Neighborhood Where You're Purchasing A Home In The Daytime And At Night

You want to go to your house and see how it is normally during the day. Check things like which cars are around, how busy is the neighborhood and what's occurring during a normal work day?

If it's possible go back around 7 p.m. to see how it is in the evenings. What is it like when everybody is home from work and school?

What are the neighborhood demographics? Who do you see in the neighborhood? Are there kids playing? Are there people walking in the neighborhood or out enjoying any parks?

What is it like in the evening time?

It's also a great idea to go to the property on the weekend to see what that is like. What are people doing in that area?

You will get a real feel for the neighborhood by visiting a property during the daytime on a weekday, during the evening on a weekday and on a weekend.

It can many times be VERY deceiving if you've only spent time at the house or in the neighborhood when you first saw that home, and maybe once more at your inspection. You may run into some "undesirable" things once you close and move in that could've been avoided prior to that.

14. Write A Love Letter

Alright, we're not talking about writing a letter to a prisoner or to an old high school sweetheart.

In this case, we're talking about writing a letter to the seller of the home you want to purchase, telling them what you love most about the house.

***Check with your Agent to see if this is permissible within your MSA/MLS... I've recently heard of some MLS areas starting to NOT allow this tactic for Fair Housing reasons.

This letter should be no more than one piece of paper long telling them how you vision your family living in the house. You want to share what excites you about the neighborhood and why you want this transaction to move forward.

This is a great thing to include with an offer ESPECIALLY when you are getting into multiple offer scenarios.

15. Auctions & Bank Sales Can Be Deceiving

Oftentimes online, you will see people marketing things like pre-foreclosures or short sales/foreclosures. Other terms to look for are HUD Homes, RSA's or Bank Owned Homes.

On the surface they can seem like a great deal.

When you really dig in, one of the main differences in these properties versus listed homes is that they are rarely move-in-ready.

Most first-time buyers, especially those who have never gone through this process, forget to calculate the cost to rehab the property to make it livable, not to mention the continued rent you're paying to live somewhere else during the rehab. You could potentially avoid having to experience what a painful, expensive and long process that can be.

So, when you're looking for a home and you see these fixer upper specials on random specialty websites... keep in mind what else would be required in order to make that distressed home your family home.

16. When Should I Talk With A Mortgage Lender?

Short answer: As soon as possible.

One of the things that I have found when I'm talking with any potential home buyer is that the first question they typically ask is, "Who should I talk to and how hard is it to get qualified?"

With that said, you need to get this process started as soon as possible because you want to know exactly what you qualify for. We can turn a pre-approval around in an hour or two... but many lenders can take days to finish it up and present any loan scenarios that might work for you.

You want to know if there's going to be any hiccups along the way. I mentioned this before, but it bears repeating... Without the Pre-Approval process completed, having a Real Estate Agent show you homes is a waste of everyone's time.

You don't want to be disappointed if you find a home you love but can't qualify for it. Getting pre-approved will prevent that.

17. What Credit Score Do I Need To Get A Mortgage?

The answer to this question changes with the constant changing of loan guidelines at the oversight and government level... so let's just toss out some "rules of thumb" that work at the time of this writing...

First, you should know this: There are THREE SCORES because there are three credit bureaus. To qualify a mortgage loan, we will typically use the MIDDLE Score. Not the Average. If there is more than one borrower on the loan, we will use the MIDDLE Score if the LOWER of the two borrowers. That score is what we will use to qualify the entire loan.

The average credit score floor (or minimum) right now is a 620. Many lenders can and will go lower for various loan products or reasons...

Somewhere between 620-640 is preferable with the scores today.

If it's REALLY LOW, and there are things that need to happen over time to clean things off and improve scores... We have a "4-month guaranteed

approval" program through our credit repair
partner. (Ask me for details)

Here is a graphic showing what your credit scores
are made up of:

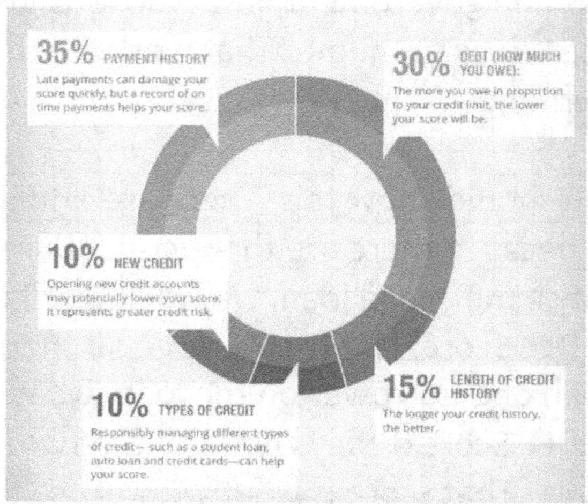

Obviously, the higher the score the better. But, as
we have seen in the past, there are some people
that unfortunately have had some hiccups. That's
OK! Everybody has had a few credit dings in their
past.

We prefer to get you up in the 620-640 range to
get a mortgage. There are some benefits to
having a higher credit score though: lower down
payment minimums, better interest rates/pricing,
better PMI factors, and better availability of loan

programs. The higher your scores, the better all of these terms will be.

Some credit manipulation tricks to consider:
- Don't close old tradelines, history matters!
- Utilization is really important. Keep your revolving balances (Credit cards, Lines of Credit, HELOCs, etc.) below 29% of the limits, but NOT Zero. Let a small balance carry from one month to the next.
- Never pay ANYTHING late.

18. What Is The Minimum Down Payment To Get A Mortgage?

The answer to this question is VERY program dependent, and will vary by loan limits in your particular part of the country. There are quite a few programs and county loan limits out there, so for a true answer, consult your favorite mortgage professional.

That said, these are the 3 most common "tiers":

There are zero down options with the VA and USDA programs. There are also the zero down state assistance programs we mentioned earlier with the silent 2nd mortgages that cover the down payment for the first mortgage.

You've also got 3.5% down payment options with the FHA program.

Then, most Conventional loans have options as low as 3% down (5% in "high price/high balance" price ranges).

19. How Much Cash Do I Need To Buy A Home?

Well, that depends on exactly what program you're applying and approved for.

Some of the fees most buyers pay at closing CAN include:

- Home appraisal (typically out of pocket and OUTSIDE of closing)
- Home inspections (typically out of pocket and OUTSIDE of closing)
- Title/Escrow closing fees
- Pre-paid taxes, insurance, HOA dues, etc.
- Third party fees

You will receive a closing cost estimate when you apply for a home loan showing you all the costs from that particular mortgage company. Each company varies slightly.

For a complete list of possible fees, and the detailed definitions of each, see the Appendix of Terms at the end of the book.

20. Should I Pay Discount Points?

Many people think that if you want to buy discount or pay discount points to buy down the rate that's going to make a big difference. You have got to look at the long term. Just because you're paying discount points to get a lower interest rate doesn't necessarily mean you're saving money. There's a cost vs. benefit analysis that GOOD lenders should be able to give you.

You have to figure out how long you will be living in the home, and how much 'savings' you can get from paying discount points.

My team and I offer EVERY applicant a Total Cost Analysis (TCA) after finishing the approval process. It shows your best scenario options and terms for multiple loan options side by side to compare. It shows immediate costs, but also costs vs. benefit OVER TIME!

I advise my clients to pay discount points or not based on cost over time analysis and I show them the difference between the return on their money vs. how long it's going to take to recoup that money when they pay for the rate buydowns.

We need to see exactly what they're going to get in return if they reduce the rate because of the discount points paid.

21. What Is The Difference Between A Fixed-Rate Mortgage And ARM Loan?

A fixed rate mortgage stays at the same interest rate for the length of the loan. Nothing changes. So, if you have it for the full term of 15, 20, 30 years it stay fixed, nothing changes on that rate.

The only thing that might change is your estimates for your tax or insurance. These can and will adjust over time, which will affect your total monthly payment here and there.

Now for an ARM or Adjustable Rate Mortgage, there will typically be a temporary FIXED period in the beginning, and then your rate can adjust after the initial fixed rate timeframe. Depending on what ARM program it might go up or down according to what the market is doing.

Each type of mortgage has its own benefits and drawbacks so it is very important that you speak with your lender and look at each type of loan to see what best fits for your unique situation.

22. What Will My Mortgage Payment Include?

Principal, interest, tax and insurance.

We often abbreviate this as PITI.

Principal - The monthly portion of the amount of the loan that you borrowed.

Interest- The charge that the bank or institution charges for lending you the principal loan amount.

Tax- The taxes charged by the local and state governments may be included here.

Insurance- The homeowner's insurance (some people call it hazard insurance) which is to cover the home and ensure that any problems or damages are able to be covered.

You can also add into this section potential PMI (Private Mortgage Insurance). This is an insurance premium required on many loan products when the down payment is less than 20% as a rule of thumb. There are monthly premium options, or paid-in-full, upfront premiums as well.

You should also factor in any HOA dues required if it applies to the home you're purchasing.

23. Can Someone Give Me Money For My Down Payment?

Yes, they absolutely can.

This is also very loan product depending as each set of guidelines details this a bit different so make sure to ask your lender how to properly account for this according to YOUR particular loan type.

Immediate family (generally parents, grandparents, children, siblings, spouses, fiances, etc.) can "GIFT" down payment funds to their family members.

It needs to be properly documented according to the guides of your loan product, but it is definitely an option...and a COMMON one. The documentation is key to ensuring that we understand exactly what those funds are for and that they are to be assigned to the down payment of the home.

Often times a signed gift letter will be required from the donor.

24. Why Should I Buy A Home Instead Of Rent?

Well we all need SOMEWHERE to live right? Somewhere to call home, put our stuff, spend our time, build memories, stay dry, eat our food, sleep, etc. etc.

Buying a home is an asset that potentially will appreciate in value. The MORTGAGE is the liability. Many of the wealthiest people in the world have most, if not all, of their worth tied to real estate.

Increasing your equity position has a few factors that contribute to it. The two main ones are YOUR on-time payments reducing your loan amount AND the market appreciation of your home (value going up due to market conditions).

At a MINIMUM, it's a forced savings account. Let's assume that you owe $200,000 on your home. You pay for 30 years and your home doesn't appreciate AT ALL, still worth $200,000 thirty years later. Well that money is yours (or your heirs). You know what you would have saved up at the end of paying rent for 30 years?! ZERO.

Obviously, that's worst-case scenario and highly unlikely as homes DO appreciate over time... but you get the savings account analogy nonetheless.

There are also tax breaks involved so you're able to write certain things off when you are purchasing a home. I'm no CPA, and don't pretend to be one... so consult one for more information on that.

Don't get me wrong... I'm a mortgage lender and I've rented. There is a time and a place for needing to rent your home... and your reasons are your own. But a long-term investment strategy it IS NOT.

Outside of the financial aspect of the Rent vs. Own debate, is the PRIDE of ownership. There is something to be said about the FEELING of owning the home you live in. It's not anyone else's. It's yours. You can paint walls whatever color you want without asking the landlord for permission.

25. How Do I Know How Much House I Can Afford?

That's why you need to talk to a reputable lender as soon as possible when you are considering becoming a homeowner. Your "affordability" is generated from your Debt to Income (DTI) ratio.

It's a simple math equation. We calculate your monthly GROSS (before taxes) income and compare that to your monthly debts to understand how much you may qualify for on a mortgage.

The debts we use in this calculation are added together, as follows: a) the potential housing payment you're about to take on, b) monthly credit card minimum payments, c) installment loan monthly payments (cars, student loans, etc.), d) monthly child support obligations, and e) any and all other monthly debt obligations that show up on your credit report.

Speaking with a loan officer sooner rather than later will help you understand where you are currently at financially and affordability-wise. You then take that figure range and you and your Real Estate agent then come up with what your possibilities are in your desired purchase area.

26. How Long Does It Take To Buy A House?

Usually it takes 20 to 40 days <u>from the time you find the home</u> until you close. Refinances can take longer. Some lenders can complete the transaction quicker, but that hinges on several factors... mainly how quickly you can perform when asked for needed documents, length of appraisal time, underwriting turn times, etc.

There could be some circumstances that come up that might delay that process but that is a general timeline that most loans are closing in at the moment.

27. What Is Earnest Money?

I told you I'd get to this!!

Earnest money is the money you put in an escrow account to show the seller you are serious about the offer.

Often, sellers don't want to accept just anybody's offer. So, an earnest money deposit is given to show good faith that the potential buyer is serious about purchasing the home.

It's typically deposited and held in either the escrow company's trust account or at the real estate brokerage where your buyer's agent works. It's then either refunded to you at closing, or it's accounted for in your transaction as part of your down payment/cash to close amount.

28. Is There A Difference Between Buying A Home To Live In And Buying An Investment Property?

Absolutely. There's a big difference between these two things, and especially in the qualifying process.

You can get up to 100% financing when you are actually looking for a primary residence. Owner occupied home purchases will get you the optimal loan terms, fees, rates, etc.

According to the bank, it's a safer bet and more secure that you are purchasing a home and living in it versus purchasing an investment property.

When you're purchasing an investment property, the bank is going to look at this from a risk point of view. If a client gets sick, gets a job transfer, loses a job, etc. the first thing they would potentially "let go of" to lower their debt load and financial burdens is NOT going to be the home they live in.

Because of the risk for the bank, investment properties typically require larger down payment minimums and will come with higher interest rate options.

Generally, investment homes require about 20% down, but 25% is better.

Strategizing if this is a good move financially is NOT for the faint of heart. Consult your financial planner, your professional mortgage lender AND your CPA, all as part of formulating a good strategy to accumulate property.

29. Condos Are An Affordable Path To Homeownership

Condominiums and townhomes are a great way to enter the homeownership market. As we briefly touched on in the first section of the book, there are some things to consider.

They are typically more affordable in both sales price and monthly costs, as much of the day to day, year to year costs of typically home ownership are SHARED amongst the community.

The right complex will still appreciate in value, perhaps not AS quickly as a single-family neighborhood, but it will still trend along with the rest of the area. With recent finance changes, condominiums are easier to finance too.

Most buyers who cannot afford a single-family home will say "I'll continue to rent, I don't want to pay HOA dues, they are a waste of money!"

I then ask, "Do you know what the HOA fee covers?" MANY HOA dues will cover water, sewer, garbage, etc. which most buyers never consider in their costs when purchasing a detached home.

Compared to the cost and maintenance of a single-family home, HOA's can be a bargain!

Condominiums and townhomes are an excellent way to start investing in real estate. You're in control of the interior and the exterior is maintained by the HOA.

Many buyers purchase a single family home and become overwhelmed with the upkeep and maintenance. Buying a home with an HOA also frees up your time.

While other homeowners are browsing the aisles of Home Depot looking for a replacement sprinkler head, you're enjoying your sparkling pool! No yardwork, exterior painting, re-roofing, etc.

Owning a condo compared to renting? There is no comparison!

With ownership you gain appreciation, equity, tax advantages and the peace of mind that you can live there as long as you want without the stress of a lease. It's truly the only way to control your long-term housing expense.

30. What Are Contingencies?

The current purchase contract in Washington is about 6 pages and when you add in each addendum for every individual contingency that you'd like to include, they get REALLY long, and there is a lot of information in there!

There are basically 2 contingencies you need to really pay attention to. If you miss one, you are out of contract, and technically, the seller can cancel your contract and sell your home to someone else while keeping your Earnest Money. An experienced agent and lender will make sure you stay on schedule.

The first major contingency is the **Property Inspection**.

The seller usually gives you between 5-15 days to order inspections and satisfy yourself as to the condition of the property.

This is the time you verify the roof doesn't leak, the sewers properly drain, the electrical systems are adequate and further research any red flags that these inspections can uncover.

Your agent will go back to the seller accepting the property as is or asking for repairs or further negotiations.

The second contingency is the **Appraisal**. It is part of your overall Financing Contingency, which essentially says that you'll make a "good faith" effort to obtain financing in a reasonable amount of time (each PSA will set a timeline for this). If after you've attempted to get a home loan, you find that you cannot… then you can cancel the purchase and get your earnest money refunded.

Your lender will order the appraisal within the first few days of the process and will get a report due date from the appraiser once the job is accepted. We will all review the appraisal, verify it came in at the sales price we offered with and requires no repairs.

In a very competitive seller's market, contingencies are a great way to make your offer better than others, without paying a higher price.

Is it very easy to shorten timelines? Shorter timelines are valuable to a seller and increases the odds of your offer being accepted.

Is it risky? Not, if it's done correctly.

An experienced agent and lender team will ensure you will not risk losing your earnest money if timelines aren't met.

The appraisal gets ordered right away, sometimes on a rush. The inspections need to be done within a few days.

31. Explore Your Down Payment Options

When buying a home, you basically need two amounts of money. One is for the down payment and the other is for closing costs. At the end, they both get lumped into an amount typically known as "Cash to Close".

Generally, closing costs are 1.5-2% of the sales price and your down payment will vary, depending on the loan type.

If you're using VA home loan benefits you will not need a down payment. Otherwise, consider these options.

401K Loan –

If you have a 401K, TSP or other retirement account, you should ask the plan administrator if you can take out a loan. Most plans allow you to borrow 50-60% of the balance and can usually set the interest rate and payment.

It is not a taxable event because it's not a withdrawal, you borrower the money from yourself. The lender could possibly count the payment against you (aka, add it as a debt and adjust your Debt to Income ratio or DTI) and lower your approval amount, so make sure to ask your lender how this will affect your approval.

IRA's do not usually allow for a loan and can only be a withdrawal.

Down Payment Assistance Programs –

As discussed previously, there are programs that are state, county or city specific that offer differing options for down payment coverage. So, for a conforming first mortgage loan, either FHA or Conventional with a 3-3.5% down payment requirement, these programs would lend you 3-4% to COVER that down payment, and would go into a 2nd lien position on your home.

These are NOT "grants" as they do need to be repaid. However, they typically carry Zero interest and you can defer payment until the end of your term. So, these 2nd mortgages just sit there silently waiting.

Lender/Realtor Commission Credits –

Technically, you cannot use lender credits for a down payment. You can, however, use the credits for closing costs, saving your cash for the down payment.

If you take a lender credit, it will come in the form of a rate credit, so you take a higher rate. You will need to look at all interest rate options to see if the higher rate is worth the extra cash at closing. Most lenders will then commit to refinancing you when rates and equity position make sense to do so down the road.

Gift Funds –

As discussed previously, you can buy a home with zero money out of pocket if you find a kind relative who has excess money lying around. This is permissible as long as a few qualifications are met. Two major things: They need to be immediate family (a distant 2nd cousin doesn't work) AND you need to intend to occupy your new home (typically this works for primary residence purchases only).

The best way to utilize gift funds is to allow the donor to leave the funds in their own bank account.

The lender will simply ask for a copy of the donor's bank statement and a letter stating this money does not have to be repaid (in other words, they're "gifting" it to you).

Intentionally left BLANK for any NOTES:

32. Let's Talk About Sewers

It's a fact, every home must have a sewer drain.

There are basically two types. A public sewer takes all the waste water from your home into the main sewer pipes under the street.

If you live in a rural area where no public sewer is available, you will have a septic tank. This is a giant tank buried in your yard where the wastewater goes and must be pumped out occasionally.

Today we're talking about public sewers which is most common.

When purchasing a home, a lateral sewer inspection is highly recommended. During the inspection phase of your purchase, you can contract a licensed plumber to send a camera down through the main drain.

The camera will show, through a video, exactly what is clear or blocked all the way to the main sewer line in the street.

This can be a particularly big problem when buying an investor remodeled home, or a flip. Flippers are known for cutting corners.
When a flipper demolishes a home, they do not cover the hole where the toilet goes, and all the construction debris can clog up the pipes. They then set a new toilet and never verify the drains are clear.

Here's the main issue: A normal property inspection does not discover this problem.

Once the unsuspecting buyer moves in and starts using all the plumbing, the construction debris can catch somewhere in the plumbing and cause sewage backups anywhere there is a drain.

This is not pleasant!

Another main reason for backups is tree roots.

When the inspection camera goes through the line, you will be able to see all the dirt, cracks and roots that can block the main line. Since it's lateral, it typically does not really drain downhill and can easily clog with debris. This is the time in your buying process where you would want to discover these issues that are, many times, never addressed in the buying process. Show the video to the seller and their agent and request repairs or renegotiate a change satisfactory to both parties.

Don't find yourself on the wrong end of a clogged drain, discuss with your agent to find a reputable and affordable option to get this inspection in addition to your structural home inspection. This small extra fee for this additional inspection that is often overlooked can save you THOUSANDS.

Once you're the homeowner... it's ON YOU!

33. Attention Military - Top 5 Reasons You Want To Use Your VA Loan Benefit

If you've served our country by being in the military, you deserve this awesome benefit!

It is the best loan out there in my opinion.

VA loans offer no minimum down payment, typically some of the lowest rates available, no private mortgage insurance (PMI) and some of the most generous underwriting guidelines.

Let's look at the top 5 reasons you should use your VA home loan benefit in a little more detail.

No Down Payment –

The national loan amount as of this writing is moving to $510,400 for the year 2020. In my tri-county area of Puget Sound in Washington State, which is consider a "high-price/high-balance" area, the loan limit for 2020 is actually $741,750!! Any LOAN AMOUNTS ABOVE these numbers are considered a JUMBO loan, and ALL the rules change. Guidelines are very different when discussing a Jumbo Loan.

No Loan Limits (NEW!) –

That previous statement regarding loan limits is true of all loan programs EXCEPT VA!! As of January 1, 2020, the VA loan limits are being removed entirely. This means that even if you are able to buy a home above your county loan limit, you can STILL do so with a zero down VA loan.

No PMI –

On MOST loan products, unless you bring in a 20% cash down payment, your lender will require you to buy Private Mortgage Insurance to cover them in case of a foreclosure.

Not with VA!

VA loan program is paid for with a funding fee (see below), a one-time cost added to the loan. If you have at least a 10% service-related disability, some or all of this fee can be waived.

This saves the average VA home buyer $300-500 a month on the payment.

Generous Credit Guidelines –

A VA loan is one of a select few options for home loans that allow you to buy a home only 2 years after a major derogatory credit event like bankruptcy, foreclosure and short sale.

You are also not penalized as heavily for having low credit scores. A 620 FICO score can still get you a good rate. Other loan programs require a minimum 680 to be competitive with rates and pricing.

Qualify For a Higher Loan Amount –

Most lenders use a debt to income ratio (DTI) to determine your ability to repay a mortgage. Not the VA!   VA loans use a residual income model. This benefits most military buyers and helps them qualify for substantially more than with other programs.

Better Interest Rates –

VA loans usually carry a lower interest rate than other programs.

Conventional loans want you to have a 680-720 minimum score or you will pay a substantially higher rate as well as higher PMI factors.

Some lenders claim they can use a 580 score... and we can, but it's really expensive!

You are better off taking a few months and improving your credit score before buying. Most VA lenders use a 620 score to get a good rate and 680+ to get an even better rate. Also, VA loans can be used more than once. Sometimes even before the original loan is paid off.

Your best bet is to talk to an experienced VA lender who can share their knowledge and direct you to an experienced agent.

The teamwork of a good agent/lender will ensure your offer gets accepted, your timelines met and have you moving into your home on time.

BONUS Reason!!!

HOMES FOR HEROES

Myself, and some Real Estate Agents that I work with in my area are approved affiliates of the Homes for Heroes program.

As described earlier in the book, we can offer incentive pricing on closing costs for active and retired military, as well as some commission rebates on the Real Estate Agent side. Depending on purchase prices, this can add up to a SIGNIFICANT amount of money in fee reductions and rebates offered if you choose to work with an approved lender.

34. 15 Year Mortgage vs 30 Year Mortgage

Many times, throughout any given week I get asked, "What is the difference between a 15-year mortgage and a 30-year mortgage"?

I usually try and lighten up the mood a little and respond with a quick, "About 180 monthly payments!" Really what our borrower is trying to determine is, does it make more financial sense to sign closing papers on a 15-year mortgage or a 30-year mortgage? So, the question I ask is, "What are you trying to accomplish by getting a 15-year loan verses a 30-year loan"?

Most of the time the answer to this question is simply that they want to pay the loan off quicker than 30 years. I am 100% fine with either loan, but the borrower needs to evaluate a few key pieces to buying this home to make sure they make the right choice.

A simple Total Cost Analysis that we send to all of our borrowers will show a few loans side by side, as well as graph out the costs/savings over time when these loans are compared. For our example today, we are going to use some simplistic figures.

We will use a purchase price of $250,000 at 3% down, with a 4.25% interest rate for a 30-year note and a 3.75% interest rate for a 15-year note.*

This is just an example and not a guarantee that either of these interest rates are attainable at the time of reading this book.

Generally speaking, if we take the $242,500 loan amount with these interest rates, we will quickly determine that the principal and interest payment for the 30-year note is $1192.50, and the payment for the 15-year note is $1,763.51, a monthly increase of $570.56. Just FYI, these figures do not account for any taxes, insurance, PMI or HOA dues.

Of course, there will be interest savings over the 15 years even though your monthly payment is higher. Significant savings actually. In this particular scenario, you'd save $55,878 in interest paid in over the 15 years by having the lower interest rate.

Visit https://mcedge.tv/1coxav to see this exact scenario and notice the graphs showing the savings over time.

HOWEVER! A completely different way of asking this question is: What ELSE can I do with that $570 if I went with the 30-year fixed and invested the difference? At a modest 2% return with compounding interest (your typically performing Money Market Account), your $570/mo. will be worth $120,652 after 15 years!!

So, going the 30-year fixed route but investing the difference, you'd be costing yourself $55,878 BUT making $120,652, which is a positive NET benefit of $64,774!!!

Signing the 30-year note can possibly allow you to build up some additional wealth and should something happen, you now have access to the funds needed to do unforeseen repairs, pay medical bills, buy a 2nd or 3rd home, etc.

In the event you already have a sizeable non-qualified account to pull from maybe the 15-year mortgage is the best way to go.

My point is this: MOST of the people who do what I do simply show you monthly payments, MAYBE a comparison in monthly payments across a few loan options, and then provide you with the debt and walk away. DON'T do that!!! Find a lender that will act as a GUIDE and SHOW you long term costs vs. savings over TIME.

HOW does the largest indebtedness I will ever take on actually FIT into my overall financial landscape?

This is a major key in what separates NORMAL lenders from the GREAT ones...

35. More Money Down?

At least a couple times a month I will get asked questions about putting more money down on a home instead of the minimum requirement.

Typically, this is a situation where a borrower has saved up money specifically because someone told them they must put 20% down. Sometimes this question comes up because someone wants to close out an old retirement account and utilize that money for a down payment.

Whatever the case may be, I like to utilize math and financial wisdom to see how best to advise a borrower in these situations... The math never lies.

Let's pretend that you have saved up $50,000 for your down payment, because you thought you needed that much.

That would provide for you a $250,000 sales price on your home ($50,000 = 20% of $250,000).

Assuming a 4% interest rate and a 30-year mortgage, that would give us a monthly payment for principal and interest of $955. Again, we don't need to factor in taxes, insurance, etc. for this example.

The next calculation for the same purchase price and interest rate would be on a 5% conventional giving us a $237,500 loan amount. Our payment is now $259 more per month. However, you now have $37,500 still liquid that you can do OTHER things with.*

*FYI, this example does not factor in the additional PMI that would need to be considered on the 5% down option.

The answer to the "More Money Down?" question depends on their whole financial picture.

If you took that same $37,500 and put it in a shoebox under your bed, each month you could go grab the extra $259 to pay your mortgage payment and you would have money in that shoe box for over about 145 months, that's over 12 years!

Obviously, that's not the best use of that cash either… A quick calculation shows us that averaging that same 2% rate of return from earlier on that $37,500 would give us $47,559.07 after those same 12 years and if we left it alone for the full 30 years that we pay on our mortgage we would have almost $68,000!

So, a good rule of thumb is to realize that on average you will only save about $5 per month for every $1000 that you put down on the mortgage.

Is it worth saving $5 per month? Of course, the answer is completely up to you, the borrower.

Just make sure, as these examples clearly show… that your lender isn't merely transactional and just simply fulfilling an order from you like you're buying a cheeseburger at McDonalds. Make sure they paint you pictures for ALL the options available to you!

I have had many people put the extra money down because they had saved the money for this specific purpose and they know their monthly budget will allow the payment at the lower amount. Totally great.

They usually fear that if they choose to keep the money they will spend it on something else and their monthly budget will be out of tune.

I have also had many families decide to use that money to start an investment account with a local financial advisor and treat the purchase of their home like an investment tool.

36. Do You Like To Gamble?

"Hey there, I was referred to you by ____________,
What is your interest rate?"

Eye roll emoji… What is so amusing to me about
this question is if I were to ask someone what
interest rate currently have on their existing
home, 80% would have no idea!

This "What is your rate?" question only ever
matters to anyone when financing the home.
Then they assume they got a good deal (or at least
the best deal possible for that point in time) and
they mentally move on. Financing a home is a
SMALL snapshot in time, and MOST lenders sadly
treat it as such.

So naturally my follow up question is usually,
"What would you like it to be?"

Our local market is pretty competitive and most
mortgage bankers in this area have virtually the
same rates (within 1/8th up or down I'd guess), so
shopping for an interest rate typically doesn't
make up for the time spent shopping.

After all, isn't the purpose of a lower rate to be a
lower monthly payment?

Here is where I let you, the borrower, make a choice. Do you like to gamble?

We can look at rates all the way down to the lower 3% range. That only means if you want that rate, you better be willing to pay for it!

So what does gambling have to do with anything?

Every rate available has a price. MOST lenders, when they say their rate to you, they're quoting what is called a "par rate". Par, meaning closest to zero, like Golf. The par rate has a price associated with it that is closest to zero out of pocket money to you, for that rate… THAT DAY! Pricing for rates can and do fluctuate day to day.

Let's define a term really quick.

A "discount point" is 1% of the loan amount.

So, 2 points would be 2%. When buying down an interest rate you use discount points. A 3.75% rate could cost you 1.35 discount points, or 1.35% of the loan amount.

In other words, you can choose to pay more closing costs up front to get a lower rate (lower than "par" anyway).

It also works in reverse. You can choose to take a higher rate, and the bank will credit you money back to be applied toward closing costs/fees.

For the next few minutes we need to determine a scenario. Completely hypothetical of course.

We found a perfect home for $235,000. We will utilize a 3.5% down payment program to give us a loan amount of $226,775 ($235,000 – 3.5% ($8,225) = $226,775)

A quick calculation from your reputable lender will show you that the difference between a 4.25% and 4.125% in your interest rate is a savings of between $16 and $17 per month.

Let's make an assumption that for every 1/8th we move of the % on an interest rate (.125%) the fee for that move is half of a point or .5%.

So, for our totally made up, fake AND in NO WAY real scenario... a 4.25% interest rate would cost you $0 in discount points, but for a 4.125% (an 1/8 difference) it would cost you half a point, or $1133.87.

Are you with me so far?

Now we need to determine how many months of saving our $16-$17 per month it will take to recover the initial cost.

So, for our mathematicians out there, we simply divide the cost of the buy down by that monthly savings ($1133.88 / $17 = 66.70).

So, for us to invest $1133.88 up front it would take us 66.70 months or just over 5.5 years.

So, the real question is: Will you be in this same house for more than 5.5 years? If yes, the buydown might make sense for you. If no, then take the par rate.

Interest Rates and the "Seller Buydown" –

Many times, the "buydown" points can be added to the loan amount and then "paid" by the Seller! This is a more complex strategy, but it can accomplish both a lower rate AND still keep the extra fee (points) for that lower rate IN YOUR POCKET.

Essentially, in the above example, you'd offer $236,500 on that same home that is being marketing for $235,000. Then you would ask the seller for a "seller credit" of $1,500 to be used toward your closing costs and buydown points. It's the same net proceeds to them, so they will typically agree.

Now you've essentially financed that $1,500 buydown point and got the lower rate… and this increased your monthly payment by around $7/mo. However, the total interest saved over time will be worth the slight increase in payment amount.

37. How Can I Best Be Prepared To Get A Home Loan

Here is where I share the 10 commandments of Home Buying. This is a very resourceful tool to anyone looking to get ready to buy a home.

In no particular order of importance:

1. Thou shalt not change jobs, become self-employed or quit your job

2. Thou shalt not buy a car, truck or van (or you may be living in it!)

3. Thou shalt not use credit cards excessively or let current accounts fall behind

4. Thou shalt not spend money you have set aside for closing costs

5. Thou shalt not omit debts or liabilities from your loan application

6. Thou shalt not buy furniture on credit

7. Thou shalt not originate any additional inquiries on your credit

8. Thou shalt not make large deposits without checking with me first

9. Thou shalt not close/change bank accounts

10. Thou shalt not co-sign for a loan with anyone

I think some of these are fairly obvious... but let's break them down just to make sure.

1. Thou shalt not change jobs, become self-employed or quit your job.

Most loan programs require a minimum of 30 days on a job, as long as you have been in that same line of employment, or education for that position before you can get a loan. The longer you have been employed in the same line of work the stronger the file. If you jump to self-employment, you will typically need 2 years' worth of tax returns to verify income. So, you likely just postponed getting a home loan by 2-3 years.

Also, the underwriting team will almost ALWAYS do a "Verbal Verification of Employment" a day or two before the close date. They'll call into your supervisor or HR and ask if you're still employed there.

2. Thou shalt not buy a car, truck or van (or you may be living in it!).

Not only will this drop your credit score due to the number of auto loan inquiries (when you buy a car, unless you specify with them, they will send your loan to several banks to get them to compete, but each will run your credit!) It could also increase your payment on this liability which would alter your DTI and possibly knock you out of being able to purchase.

3. Thou shalt no use credit cards excessively or let current accounts fall behind.

The underwriting team will always pull a soft pull credit report a day or two before closing to ensure debts, and monthly obligations have not increased.

4. Thou shalt not spend money you have set aside for closing costs.

The loan officer will turn in bank statements to show stability of savings account and proof of funds to close, if you spend that money you can rest assured that your loan will not close on time.

5. Thou shalt not omit debts or liabilities from your loan application.

We do run your credit and will include everything we see on that report. The most common ones that are missed because they don't show on a credit report are a) child support payments, and b) 401k loans that you pay back out of your paychecks. If you omit them, when the debt is discovered during the loan process, the underwriting team will question why it was omitted and the loan process will likely start over. Just include it ALL!

6. Thou shalt not buy furniture on credit.

Just wait until you close on the house. It's better that way.

7. Thou shalt not originate any additional inquiries on your credit.

New inquiries on credit makes underwriters think there is new debt. They will ask for a letter of explanation detailing why that inquiry is there and was any new debt incurred? Again, just wait until you close on the house. It's better that way.

8. Thou shalt not make large deposits without checking with your lender first.

Large deposits are always suspicious. We are speaking here of the "unmarked" type, such as Cash/Check/ATM deposits, or large incoming transfers. Paychecks or direct deposit are obviously fine. Check with your loan officer to see what the definition of large deposit is on the loan program you are using for your home purchase.

9. Thou shalt not cancel/change bank accounts.

Why would you want to change banks in the middle of the largest financial transaction of your life? If you hate your current bank that much, change after we close on your new home.

10. Thou shalt not co-sign for a loan with anyone.

Co-signing on a loan now makes you liable for that loan as well. So now we must start over with this new debt on your application.

38. Prepare Early & Seek The Advice Of A Trusted Mortgage Advisor

I feel like I've mentioned this a few times already?

When buying a home, you want to make sure everything is lined up the best you possibly can. Do not start shopping, or even looking at homes until you have a few pieces of information lined up.

First, identify what your maximum monthly payment is, including taxes and insurance, that your budget will allow. If you don't have a budget, try making one! There's a ton of free help on this through "the Google".

Knowing this number is more important than knowing how much of a house you can qualify to buy. If your maximum monthly payment is $2,000 you will not be able to buy a $600,000 home.

Different loan programs have different guidelines on how much you can pay for your mortgage based on the amount of income you earn.

This is called your front-end debt to income ratio.

The goal here is to establish a price range of homes that you will feel comfortable with paying for each month. Exceeding this threshold can get VERY uncomfortable, which is not where we want any of our clients to be.

After you have determined what your monthly budget will allow in a payment, start gathering a few needed documents. I recommend starting a file folder on your computer, or paper copy if you prefer. Start saving items to this file so that you can quickly upload them to the loan file electronically or email them to your loan officer.

Typically, most loan programs will need 2 years' worth of W2's used to determine the income. (Tax returns for Retired or Self-Employed borrowers)...

We will need your most recent 30 days' worth of paycheck stubs from everyone on the loan application as well as the most recent 2 months of bank account statements.

Ideally this is a checking and savings account where the money for closing is being kept.

If you are applying for a VA loan, there is an additional document needed called the Certificate of Eligibility. Most lenders can obtain this for you if you do not have one, they will just need your DD-214 to get the COE from the VA.

If you are paying or receiving child support, we will need the documents (Divorce decrees and Child Support orders) showing a current status, especially if you are using this as part of your income on the application.

If we are using funds from your 401(k) for down payment and closing cost then you'll need to provide those statements as well. They're typically quarterly statements and will need to be accompanied by a document from your 401k provider called "Terms of Withdrawal".

Finally, if you are receiving any social security or disability income, retirement funds, etc. we would need the documents showing the monthly amount received (sometimes called "Award Letters"). Typically, we will need copies of your tax returns for these streams of income as well.

Utilize the file folder recommendation mentioned earlier and send only what is needed at the time you sign the home purchase contract. You should also understand that delays in receiving needed documents could delay the loan process.

In conclusion, I think the biggest thing when anybody is purchasing a home is to get pre-approved first. ALL professional Real Estate Agents will agree.

What we typically see most people do is to talk to a Realtor first. They want to ask the Realtor all of their questions about the home buying process, neighborhoods and payments when they haven't even found out if they can qualify for a mortgage... and if so, how much?

I tell people, "The best thing you can do before you go and get your family super excited looking at homes you want to purchase is to make sure that you're qualified first. Do that before you get into a Realtor's car and have them showing you homes."

39. Zillow

I get this question a lot so I wanted to clear something up for anyone reading this. Zillow has its place. But there are some things you should know!

Zillow first and foremost, is a "lead aggregator". It is NOT a place where you should "online shop" for homes. It doesn't show you every home for sale in your given search area. It relies on Agents to post their listings to be viewed on their site.

Next, the Real Estate Agents AND Lenders PAY to be in their site and receive "leads".

Finally, they recently got into the buying and selling real estate business. AKA, they're competing with you as a buyer AND they're competing with your real estate agent.

Enough said?

40. Bank vs. Banker vs. Brokerage

Banks

Banks are typically local brick and mortar financial institutions that offer mortgages as well as traditional banking services such as checking/savings accounts, lines of credit, and Credit Cards. Local banks are in the business to lend; as a matter of fact, the law requires they use a percentage of their deposits for lending purposes. Any interest a bank earns from a loan is used to lend money for other types of loans such as: auto loans, personal loans and mortgages.

Mortgage Bankers

Mortgage Bankers can be thought of as a one-stop Mortgage shop. With access to lenders such as Fannie Mae, Freddie Mac, Wells Fargo and Chase, bankers are able to offer a vast array of home loan programs such as Conventional, Jumbo, FHA, VA and USDA.

Unlike banks, mortgage bankers concentrate solely on mortgage lending. Mortgage bankers typically employ in-house underwriters and loan processors which translates into accelerated processing and underwriting timelines and smoother closings.

Mortgage Brokers

Mortgage Brokers are federally licensed firms or individuals who sell loan programs on behalf of lenders. Mortgage brokers facilitate your search for the most suitable mortgage product and structure your loan to suit your financial goals. Mortgage brokers do not underwrite any loans – every loan is sent to the lender for underwriting. Additionally, it is the lender, not the mortgage broker, which provides the funds for your loan.

In case you're curious... I am a Mortgage Banker AND a Mortgage Broker. The best of BOTH worlds!!!

Are You Ready To Get Started?

Reach out and let's chat...

Sean Antonius (NMLS #1552487)

425.681.8075

SeanAntonius.com

Equal Housing Lender

Appendix A – Glossary of Terms

Loan Estimate –

An estimate of all closing fees including pre-paid and escrow items as well as lender charges; this must be given to the borrower within 3 days after submission of a full loan application.

APR – Annual Percentage Rate –

A measure of the cost of credit expressed as a yearly rate. It includes interest as well as other charges. Because all lenders, by federal law, follow the same rules to ensure the accuracy of the annual percentage rate, it provides consumers with a good basis for comparing the cost of loans, including mortgage plans. APR is a higher rate than the simple interest of a mortgage.

Title Insurance –

Insurance that protects the lender against any claims that arise from arguments about ownership of the property, it is also available for homebuyers. Additionally, it is an insurance policy guaranteeing the accuracy of a title search protecting against errors.

Underwriting –

The process of analysing a loan application to determine the amount of risk involved in making the loan; it includes a review of the potential borrower's credit history, income and employment as well as a judgment of the property value (appraisal).

Escrow –

Escrow assures that the lender releases the home purchase funds at (or about the same time) the deed is recorded to reflect new ownership. An escrow account is a separate account where the lender puts a portion of the monthly payment each month to ensure the taxes and insurance are paid on time.

ALTA Settlement Statement –

Also known as the "Master Statement" or "Closing Statement". This document itemizes all closing costs and must be given to the borrower at or before closing (typically at the final signing appointment with escrow). Some items that appear on the statement include: Real estate commissions, loan fees, discount points, and escrow amounts.

Document Recording –

After closing a loan, certain documents are filed and made public record. Discharges for the prior mortgage holder are filed first. Then the deed is filed with the new owner's and mortgage company's names.

Appendix B – Closing Costs/Fee Details

Processing Fee – A processing fee is a fee to cover the cost of processing your mortgage application. Processing a file includes the collecting and reviewing of documents needed for loan approval. In addition to collecting and reviewing, the processor will assemble a package of all documents from the borrower and all 3rd parties of the transaction to submit to underwriting for approval.

Underwriting Fee – The Underwriting fee are those associated with an underwriter reviewing your application and determining if the lender is willing to provide you with a loan and under what terms. The lender will review a number of factors including your assets and liabilities, income, credit history and property appraisal.

MERS Registration Fee – The Mortgage Electronic Registration System is an online search platform that allows a lender to document the transfer of a loan between different loan servicers without having to record a new assignment of deed.

Appraisal Fee – The Appraisal Fee is assessed by a 3rd party to send an appraiser out to inspect and determine the value of the subject property. This is typically a fee that will be paid OUTSIDE of your closing costs and is paid directly to the appraisal company.

Credit Report Fee – The Credit Report Fee is assessed by a 3rd party to pull a copy of your credit report. This fee also pays for any updates to your credit report during your loan process, Social Security Verification and Tax Transcripts. This fee will be estimated until closing documents are sent and the exact amount charged throughout the loan process will then be assessed.

Flood Certification Fee – This fee is assessed by a 3rd party to determine if the property is located in a FEMA flood maps zone. If the home is located in a flood zone, proof of flood insurance must be provided.

Tax Service Fee – This is assessed by a 3rd party to monitor the payment of the property taxes. This fee is to ensure the property taxes are paid on time 2x annually (location dependent). This gives the lender reassurance that there will not be a lien placed on the home due to taxes not being paid.

Mortgage Insurance – This is required if less than 20% of the sales price is put down for the down payment. This insurance protects the lender, not the borrower, in case of a default. For Conventional financing, mortgage insurance can either be assessed as a monthly payment OR a lump sum that is either paid upfront, or financed into your loan. For FHA financing, an Upfront Mortgage Insurance Premium (UFMIP) AND a monthly mortgage insurance payment will be assessed. This also applies to a refinance if there is less than 80% equity in the home.

Prepaid Interest – Interest is paid in advance at closing to keep you up to date on interest due. As interest incurred is typically paid in the following month's payment (aka, mortgage interest is paid one month in ARREARS), the interest for the time between closing and the beginning of the month must be paid.

Homeowner's Insurance Premium – This is required to cover possible damages to your home in the event that a fire or other damages occur. The first year's premium is paid at closing.

Property Taxes (Reserves) – Property taxes are a tax that is assessed by your county on the value of the property or home. $1/12^{th}$ of the yearly taxes will be collected each month in your mortgage payment and held in an escrow (or impound) account. The Property tax RESERVES are collected to ensure the correct amount of funds will be in your escrow account by the time taxes are due (April & October in our market). The months collected will change based on the month of the loan closing date.

Aggregate Adjustment – There is a minimum and maximum dollar amount which can be held in an escrow account at a time. This adjustment will be the adjustment to ensure that the correct funds are being collected. The adjustments will typically be a credit, though, it COULD also be a cost.

Escrow Fee – The Escrow fee is assessed by the Title/Escrow Company or attorney for facilitating the closing and disbursement/allocation of all funds. They handle the payoff of the current loan on the home, conduct the preparation of the closing AND signing of final documents, and handle the transfer of monies.

Lender's Title Insurance – This fee is assessed by the Title Company and covers the costs of assuring the lender that you own the home and lenders mortgage becomes a valid lien.

Owner's Title Insurance (Applies to Purchases Only) – This is assessed by the Title Company and protects the homeowner in the event that someone challenges ownership of the home. This is a fee paid by the Sellers in a purchase transaction.

Recording Fee – Government recording charges are fees assessed by the state and/or local government agencies for legally recording your deed, mortgage note and other documents related to the home purchase. This fee is charged by the local county's recording office.

Discount Points (or "Buydown" Points) – These are a way to reduce your interest rate. These are a one-time charge that will be paid at closing as a part of your closing cost to the lender. Points are expressed as a percentage of the loan amount with one point equalling one percent. For example: You pay .231 in points for a rate at a $200,000 loan amount, you would pay $462.

Lender Credits – Credit received from the lender for a rate chosen above market value. Lender Credits are applied to the total closing costs to help reduce the amount required from the borrower. Lender credit cannot be applied to down payment.

Condo Cert Fee – This confirms that the HOA has been turned over to the occupants by the developer and answers some crucial questions that pertain to the developments financing qualifications. Investors have specific requirements for financing including number of owner-occupied versus non owner-occupied units, no overabundance of units owned by one entity, no hotel like front desk, etc.

Just to name a few. There are MORE!

www.ingramcontent.com/pod-product-compliance
Lightning Source LLC
Chambersburg PA
CBHW071526150726
48000CB00002B/697